1200 DEGREES
TURN UP THE HEAT AND SURFACE

ILKA MURRAY

Published by Leading Through Living Community, LLC

Copyright © 2017 Ilka Murray

Edited by David M. Good

Bible references quoted from the Message Bible and King James Version of the Holy Bible.

All Rights Reserved. No part or portion of this publication may be reproduced, stored in a retrieval system, or transmitted in any form or by any means - electronic, mechanical, photocopying, recording, or otherwise - without the express written consent of the author.

For information:

Leading Through Living Community LLC
6790 W. Broad Street Suite 300
Douglasville, GA 30134

ISBN-10: 0-9983482-9-5
ISBN-13: 978-0-9983482-9-2

1200 DEGREES CONTENTS

	Introduction	5
1	Rising Out of the Ashes	9
2	Slow Down & Cool Off	23
3	Rest: The Often Neglected Secret	41
4	Friends in the Fire	53
5	Change State	65
6	P2 = Pressure + Purpose	75
7	Surface	85

INTRODUCTION

Have you ever felt like you have been doing everything right, you started to advance in many areas of your life, and you wake up one day and ask yourself: What happened to me? Where am I? How did I get here? How am I going to get out? You just could not wrap your mind around the fact that things were far from perfect. You remember starting with a vision, but now it seems a little blurry. What a feeling that is to know that you are not where you had dreamed of being, and the road back is not an option, but the road forward seems so far out of reach that you don't know where to begin. This book is a companion to your successful journey in life. God has designed a path for you. It's hard to see our greater life beyond what we see every day in our lives. When you allow God to reveal what has been concealed, you become aware that there is a greater version of yourself waiting to be expressed in every area of your life. God has designed a path for each of us.

Did you know in order for a piece of metal to be refined, a temperature of 1200 degrees must be present during this process? I know that in the courses of life, transitional moments can cause the heat of life to be present. Most of the time we run from heat, but in order for your true design to be experienced, a transformational process will need to take place.

Gold, dug out from deep in the Earth in the gold mines around the world, looks nothing like the gold around your neck, on your wrist or on your finger(s). Gold from the earth, is infiltrated with impurities. The oldest remedy of refining gold is through fire. Over 1000 degrees

Celsius is used to purify gold.

You want your life to resemble a fine

piece of gold jewelry? You have to go through the refining fire. The next time you are faced with a transitional life moment, remind yourself that you are being refined at 1200 degrees.

One thing I have learned in life is when I refuse God's way, I end up taking a U-turn and going back to God anyway.

DEGREE ONE

RISING OUT OF THE ASHES

It is very easy to find yourself out of place and in trouble. Sometimes life can knock the breath out of us and we find ourselves in a moment in time that is totally opposite to what we first imagined our lives to be. The word of God shares with us about which road we should be traveling on in order to be successful in life. Mathew 7:13-14 states that the right road is narrow, but the broad road leads to destruction. It is not always easy to stay on a road that is winding and narrow. In order for life to make sense and successful for you, the road you travel must be so narrow that only you and God can fit on it. Why? As long as you travel with the crowd you will get lost in the crowd if you don't know yourself first. Traveling the narrow road allows you to focus on you through the view that God has of you. When we travel with the crowd, it allows us to pick up traits from other people that we might like, that may be appealing and good, just not for us. In order to win in your life, you have to do it leading with who you are organically, not who society has built you up to be. Imagine that you are on your way home on a dark road in the middle of the night. Your eyes are heavy with sleep and you have three more hours of road in front of you. You open the windows, hoping that the fresh air rushing through will hit your eyelids and wake you up. Maybe you are the 5-Hour-Energy type and you are on your third bottle. You turn up the music and start vibing to the beat. As you're moving and singing to the top of your lungs, you become unaware of the time you have left and get lost in the story that is being told to you through the rhythm of the drums and power of the voice behind the music. No matter how you work to change the atmosphere of tiredness, your body seems to be winning the battle. You now find yourself in a moment that offers a choice to push past the boundaries of tiredness and keep going or to give in.

This story is a parallel picture of your life. The path for your life has already been prepared and not going anywhere. If you veer off, you veer off. It is still there, just get back on the same way you would if you veered off the road and into the bushes that border the lane you're driving on. God has not changed His mind about your destiny and it's important that you are confident in that knowledge. It is going to get hot and you may even get burned. At times you're going to find yourself tired and you're going to run into fear. But you can rise from the ashes, heal from every wound, and be energized to achieve great things in your future. Philippians 4:13 states whatever I have, wherever I am, I can make it through anything in the one who makes me who I am. You can push past any challenge because God's strength is with you and you are designed to win. There is a story in the Bible about David and Bathsheba is about rising from ashes. You may have heard the story before, but I want to tell it again to compare it with your contemporary life.

David was the second king of Israel. While the Israelites were at war with the Philistines, David finds himself walking around the palace roof peering into the window of a beautiful woman taking a bath. He sends one of his assistants to go retrieve her. Now, you might ask, "Why did she come to see this fine man knowing that she was a married woman?" You must know that when the king commanded something, you obeyed or you risked your life. It's funny how in reverse, when we obey God's layout for our life we gain our life, when we refuse to accept His offer to come to Him and live out life the way He designed for us, we risk our life. One thing I have learned in life is that when I refuse God's way, I end up taking a U-turn and going back to God anyway. Why not save time and hardship by starting this next chapter of your life with God. Life is so much better with Him. The king's words were final and she risked death if she disobeyed. This woman was in her proper place, she understood the meaning of her decisions according to her lifetime and settings so she went. Since we mentioned this part, how about the part that David had no business checking out Bathsheba. He was supposed to be at war along with the other soldiers, but he was idle and walking around on the palace's roof top.

Fast-forward: Bathsheba is her name and she sleeps with David that night. She gets up and collects herself and goes home. Where is her husband? Uriah is out fighting the war with everyone else.

The Bible does not mention it, but I am sure that it is about a month or two later and Bathsheba finds out that she is pregnant. She tells King David. Now sit and think for a minute…. If you are Bathsheba, what should you do or if you are David what should you do? It is getting extremely hot. David and Bathsheba are in deep. David calls for Uriah to come home from the war and talk to him.

David did not have a moment of remorse, nor did he plan to confess. His corrupt plans continued. In the 21st Century, DNA testing is performed thousands of times a day. But, there was no such thing back in those days. David is hatching a scheme to put the baby on the husband. There is a big problem: Uriah is a man of principle and character.

Doesn't that make you mad when you think you have a good idea, but to make it work someone else has to agree to it? This was David's dilemma. Uriah would not go home and sleep with his wife. He ate and talked with David that evening, but he slept outside with the other servants. When David questioned why, he was told that Uriah did not feel comfortable about relaxing at home with his wife while his peers were outside in tents waiting to go back to war.

David's mind starts working again. I want to mention a very important principle right here. This story is taking place in II Samuel, but back in I Samuel, God said that David was a man after His own heart. I know you don't think that all the mess we get ourselves into escapes the mind of God. Know that it does not. David is getting in very deep! His situation is catching on fire and not a good fire.

David's thoughts are spinning and he is adding to his plot to deceive. The next evening, he sets a plan in motion starting with Uriah. David gives Uriah a taste of his life by wining and dining him, but underneath the feast was a plan of defeat. David gets him drunk. Sometimes the very thing you are committed to is the very thing destroying you. Maybe a drunken man will want to lay with his wife.

Uriah had not changed his stance. He wanted to be with his peers and did not want to go home. He slept again at the door of the king with the other men; David is at his wit's end.

I cannot imagine what in the world was going through the mind of Bathsheba. I don't care if I had to lay with the king, how am I going to pull this off on my husband, a baby conceived while he is out in battle?

David is thinking. I can see him pacing back and forth in the middle of the night trying to figure it all out. His final plan is coming clear to him. Uriah must die! David sent word to the top man to put Uriah on the front line so that he could be killed on the battlefield. He sent this word by letter, a letter carried by the intended target, Uriah. The plan is set and carried out as planned: Uriah is killed.

After Bathsheba mourns for her husband, David sends for her and they are married. I guess he probably thought his plan worked and he could move on with his life. **God does not work like that**. What is done in the dark comes into the light, eventually. **God sees everything and through revelation, you will see it as well**. Before we continue with David and his tangled life, I was to remind you of why you want the purifying fire of God to be alive in your life.

Fire brings two elements into your life:
1. Fire brings heat. Heat purifies what is no longer valuable. When new grass is needed, the old grass is burned to the dirt layer. When a dead fish needs to be cooked, fire is applied and the nutrients are then experienced by those who desire it or need it.
2. Fire brings light. Light always reveals what has been hidden or unseen. In our lives, the light of Jesus brings forward the true design of our destiny. Light allows us to see our image in the metal, our lives. Light

allows you to see better than seeing in the dark.

Now back to David.

God sent word to David by way of the prophet Nathan. Nathan tells David a story of a rich man that takes advantage of a poor man. The rich man is said to have taken the things that belong to the poor man. David despises the rich man and tells Nathan that the rich man should die. He finds out that the rich man in the story is him. Nathan tells him that the baby he had with Bathsheba will die for this sin.

What a hot mess! The baby dies. But you must remember that **God's plans always trump your plans**. No matter how high the flame, you are being refined. You probably thought that God chooses the way to purify you and you are just a victim of His heavy-handed dealings. Not so! It's time to dismantle this way of thinking. The only way to stay on your path is to make some wrong turns. There is no such thing as a perfect life on this earth. Perfection in your eyes is not like perfection in God's eyes. His ways are nothing like our ways (Isaiah 55:8). Even in trying to do all good things, you will get caught up in some bad situations. Thank God for His grace.

Grace to me has been His presence during my refining process, the power that goes beyond my ability, and allows me to experience in my challenging moments. **Grace enables me to win even though I keep failing. It is encouragement laced in my doubts, the strength highlighted in my weakest moments and the happiness that I can see even if it's a mile away.** Why do you think that we have the scripture that says all things work together for the good …? (Romans 8:28) It really does not matter how bad things look, you are being refined; that is the good. The good is the greater parts of who you are underneath, not the greatest parts of life that are currently piled on top. *1200 degrees* is about unveiling the real you in spite of all the choices that were made that did not empower your destiny.

I know what it's like to start planning on your passions, doing the pre work, getting started and finding your flow, then BAM, hitting a brick wall. *What was that?* I ask myself, having no clue. But one thing that is for certain, God always presents His plan again and allows me to be a part of the execution process. **Things always work out so much better when** God is leading me in every area of my life.

Just because David made a whole bunch of wrong turns God did not fire him from his post nor did He take His hand off of David's life. After all, David and Bathsheba's next child ended up being the wisest man of the Bible, King Solomon. He was named Solomon by his parents but called Jedidiah by Nathan the prophet, which means loved of the Lord.

You made some mistakes and got burned. **It really is okay. Really! It is ok**. There is life in the ashes. David repented when confronted with his sin. David fasted and pleaded with God when his first baby got sick. When God said it was over, it was over. David got up and ate when the baby died. **You do not have to stay down in your mess. The original plan is still good**.

Get up and collect yourself. Take off the sooty clothes and get fresh. There are brand new mercies every day (Lamentations 3:22). Why do you think there is such a thing as grace and mercy? No, you do not take advantage of grace and mercy, but they are there for you. Use them. It could have been a so-called good plan or a knowingly evil one. You messed up! And…?!

You can rise from the ashes.

Life is designed to bring you closer to your CREATOR.

DEGREE TWO

SLOW DOWN & COOL OFF

As I mentioned in the introduction, a refiner of precious metals sets his flame higher than 1200 degrees to draw out the impurities that are natural to things coming out of the earth. Comparing yourself to the precious metal of gold is a huge undertaking. Going through the refiner's fire is no joke. It is hot! It is so hot that most people choose to stay where it's cool. What a refiner is looking for in the gold is his reflection. God is doing the same thing. **When we allow God to refine us, we allow Him to dust off, wash off, and bring the heat until He sees what He created.** His image, His likeness, in His creation - that is <u>you</u>. I used to ask God does it bother Him to see me going through hard times in my life. I believe that it doesn't make God feel great to see us struggle, He loves us more than we can imagine, but I believe that it also gives Him excitement because He knows we already have in us everything we need to get through it all and come out winning. When the refiner sees his image in the piece of metal he chose to put into the fire, that tells him that the process has been completed. This is the same process that God takes you through. God has no desire to destroy you, although it may feel that way when you are in the fire. In this chapter, I want to walk you out of the troubled path that you may find yourself on when you try to run out of the fire before you have been refined.

In the previous chapter, I mentioned the story of David. I shared with you that David, like us at times, tried to run out of the fire in every direction that he could find, only to find himself still in it when his plans failed. You may discover that your plan(s) actually did not completely fail, but they did not bring you to the desired results. This is because you have not yet come to the realization that you are not really in control. God is a just God. You are a free moral agent and can make your own choices. But life is designed to bring you closer to your creator. No matter where you find yourself, God is waiting there with open arms. He wants you to be successful more than you want to be successful.

There is a scripture that says that it is God's good pleasure that you have His kingdom (Luke 12:32). His kingdom is the invisible world that operates in the heart of every believer that wants to live in the fullness of God promises. The problem is that you have to sell all of your plans to live in the better plan that God has prepared for your life. Your plan is probably expensive, but God's plan is free. Well, not exactly. It will cost you your faith. The truth is you use faith every day. You choose to believe and place your hope into something. Whether it is in God's plan for your life and His strategies to get you there or not . That is only something you can answer. I want to offer this to you at this point of the book. **Challenge yourself for the next 90 days to ask God every morning, what does He want you to do today.** It's a simple question filled with great adventure when you listen to God's voice and look for Him in all parts of your day. In life, we experience a daily combo that is made up of three elements:

    1. Problem
    2. Solution
    3. Implementation of change

Along with those elements are four companions.

    1. Mental state
    2. Emotional state
    3. Physical state
    4. Spiritual state

In every situation, you must identify the problem, which requires transparency and truth. Ask God to shine light on the solution, and implement the change, which will require obedience to God and consistency. In this process you will have to make a shift mentally, emotionally, physically, and spiritually. Nothing advances in life without growth in these areas.

Personally, I went through some tough health problems. Not to take anything away from the woman with the issue of blood, mine can't even begin to compare to what she went through, but her tenacity to see the greater in her to come out is what assisted me in my journey. (Mark 5:25) I felt like her. I went from doctor to doctor, diagnosis to diagnosis, medication to medication. It all came back to nothing; I was still in poor health. Have you ever found yourself in a cycle of habits or experiences with no end in sight? That was me for years concerning my health. Never-ending answers from doctors that said they didn't know what was going on. The ongoing saga of choices that lead me to nowhere. It was the nightmare that never ended. Another day, same storyline. But then one day...

I pray that you will wake up to your "one day" soon, and I am more than confident that you will, just like I did.

God's grace stepped in, in the form of a referral to a holistic doctor. He did a battery of tests and came back with the results. My health was in my hands. My bad health was the problem, God directed me to the solution through the doctor and his directions, and now it was time for me to do my part to implement the change. I had to completely change my eating habits. In the process I felt alive; I have more good days than bad ones, lost over twenty pounds and had to get a new wardrobe. Thank you God for the added bonus. I can talk about healing and give hope to those who are in pain like I was.

I was in real trouble. I know you

understand how that feels. But, I got a surge of courage when I was given hope. I did not have to resign to die and leave my two young children. I committed my way to God's will and I received what I desperately desired. This is not the story of overnight success but the story of God's grace and me receiving more than I asked for.

You should always have a plan, but never neglect to remember that God has to be the leader. It is sad when I see someone running in cycles because he/she does not want to deviate from their plan. Living in God's plan is a narrow way. The New Living Translation Bible says in Psalms 37:5, "Commit everything you do to the Lord. Trust Him and he will help you." That's His promise to you. **If you commit to following the guidelines He offers, you cannot help but be successful.** You have to remember: what He is offering you is not a product from an infomercial that you watch at 2 am sitting in bed while eating your favorite snack. What He offers is a path of life that is designed to highlight the best you! Jeremiah 29:11 says, *"I know the plans I have towards you declares the Lord, plans to not harm you, but plans to give you a hope and a future!"* (emphasis added) It simply comes down to this:

Do you choose His plans?

Every day, every challenging moment that rises up, the question remains the same, do you choose His plans or not? Do you choose to live life with God as the lead or not? Don't start getting into the breakdown of how you don't see a way out of where you are right now. **Don't fall into the pit of excuses of why you have to fix everything first before you can move forward on His plans.** Throw that out the window. All God wants is Him as your choice and the commitment to trust Him during the detangling of everything that is currently tangled. Don't give in to the tangled web by adding another troubled situation. **Choose to live differently today!**

There's the story of a young girl who was very intelligent. Helen was accepted by at least three Ivy League colleges. There was, however, one problem, she did not want to follow in her mother's footsteps. She felt the pull to become a lawyer, but wanted her independence. She wanted her own career. She set out to become a psychologist.

Helen did very well and was on course to complete her doctorate. Two years before this time, she knew that she had made the wrong decision. Pride was getting the best of her and she would not admit her error. In the middle of her internship, she admitted that she had been traveling down the wrong road. Of course, psychology is an excellent field of study, but it was not the field that she was gifted to operate in. Why do we keep choosing what we don't like? This happens daily in our lives. We choose in pleasing others or our imagination of what we think we want. But, in the deepest parts of our hearts we know it's not what we desire. She was supposed to be studying to become a lawyer. She knew it before she entered her first year of undergrad.

All the money that was spent on schooling seemed wasted. You might say that it will never be wasted. Maybe not, but she knew that she was doing something that was wrong for her. God has a plan that cannot be shaken. Helen went on to become a lawyer. All things do work out for good, but life can be so much simpler if we would stop and slow down when we are in the fire.

A great singer from the 80's, Angela Bofill, was struggling with her finances in 2005. As she was in the process of moving from her home, she had a stroke. A year later she had another stroke. All hopes of ever singing again were seemingly lost. After several years of therapy, she began to walk and talk again and could go home. Her sister moved in to help her with daily life. Her manager began a thought process on her behalf that would propel her into the next phase of her life. He thought about what she could do and around 2012, she returned to the stage talking to audiences about her life with stars performing the songs that made her great. You must know this, that your gift is broad and can be delegated in many different functions. If you have a gift of teaching, you can teach music, you can teach in a classroom setting, online, through writing, or dance. Never limit your gift to one area of use. As long as you're operating in the gift, the external function really doesn't matter.

It is not a lack of faith that causes you to ask, "What if my situation does not change?" The only thing that is guaranteed to change in your life is the things that you have the power to change. I will not begin to name the things that you may be wrestling with that are aggravating to you. These are the same things that God may be using to guide you to your next step. Everything is working to keep you where you should be. Am I walking in my healing? Of course I am! Do I get sick, still? Of course I do! But how I choose to think about ailments, is what keeps me alive and winning. I know that God says in His word that as a righteous person that I will be afflicted, or challenged, over and over again (Psalms 34:19). How the afflictions are going to come is out of my control. You live knowing God and loving Him with all of you: heart, soul, and mind. If you do this, then you totally trust Him, even in sickness, loneliness, despair, etc.

You walk in faith no matter what. What you are supposed to say to the afflictions is, "So!" You do not live in your emotions, you live in your faith. Every situation you get into, you keep referring back to God and keep it moving. He said you are healed, so you are healed, no matter what you feel or think. Faith is the substance of what you hope for (Hebrews 11:1). He promised deliverance from ALL afflictions. Fire is meant to be hot; it burns out impurities. The refiner keeps the precious metal in the fire for a while and then takes it out to see its progress. How are you progressing? It's unreal to think that you will never be down. That is what your praise is for, "...the garment of praise for the spirit of heaviness...." (Isaiah 61:3).

Heaviness is that weighted down feeling. It's that feeling that makes you feel that there is no way out of a situation. When you get like this, you must remember that there is power in your praise. Do not stay at home under your covers. Get around others that can encourage you. You do not have to share with anyone if you are not ready, but do not neglect your praise. The devil is always busy and takes joy in your isolation. When ten lepers came to Jesus to be healed, he told them to go and show themselves to the priest (Luke 17:14). As they went they were healed. They could have stayed in their place outside the gates of the city as was the rule. But they came knowing that their action would bring results. They requested pity from Jesus and received cleansing. So, if this happened way back then, what do you think will happen in the 21st Century? Jesus was still walking on the earth then, but He promised greater things when He left to be with His Father (John 14:12). Do not live in a state of despair when what you need, God has.

 Instead of being down, try to process what's happening in your life a little slower and give time for God's answer to be revealed. The part that needs to slow down is your thoughts. When the refiner gives you a break from the fire, do not worry about going back in the fire; I promise you that this will happen. But, put your mind at rest and know that God has your best interest. You must learn how to embrace change. Life catches us by surprise, not God. Some things are just meant to happen. **Either way, God uses it all: the good, the bad, and the ugly to bring out your best.** When something happens that you did not expect, embrace it. This is God's gift to you. He knew the road that you would take before you were born (Jeremiah 1:8). You may not have control over what happens, but you have control of how you respond to what happens. Your response process must go through the refinement process. **How you reacted in the past to challenging moments will not be the same response in your future days.** You must train yourself to be at ease with what's going on and in hopes of coming out with victory. An elder in our church shared a journal entry one day and it was great. She asked God to help her manage life's changes by correcting "deceptive highs and debilitating lows!" Balance is God's gift to you to equal out your life.

He will never leave you with more (-) negatives than (+) positives. You will always smile at the end.

Some of the greatest scriptures in the New Testament were written by the Apostle Paul while he was locked up in a Roman prison. He learned how to be content in every situation: whippings, disappointments, imprisonments, etc. What you must practice is doing what you can do. You are never left helpless. There is always something left in your hand, but slow down and gather your thoughts. Being content and patient go together. Do not neglect either one of them.

I will end here with this thought, patience is the very thing that has the greatest reward, **"... let patience have her perfect work, that you may be perfect and entire, wanting nothing."**

Whatever you need, God's got it.

He will never leave you with more (-) negatives than (+) positives.

DEGREE THREE

REST: THE OFTEN NEGLECTED SECRET

Why are some people afraid of the word rest? Is it because of the phrase, "Rest in Peace?" Maybe resting is associated with being lazy. Whatever the reason, rest is a promise to all believers, but is a neglected secret. **Rest does not mean stop.** It means to re-focus mentally, enhance you faith spiritually, and adjust physically. I heard someone once say that "God never rested, so why should we?!?" I guess that goes for the devil too. I want to explain something to you that will revolutionize your life if you put it into practice.

God promised all believers a time of rest. The way He made the heavens and the earth and rested on the seventh day was an example of how we should live. Constant movement, seven days a week, twenty-four hours a day and three hundred and sixty-five days a year is how we live today. What kind of example is that to a nonbeliever who is looking for a way out of their current life? There is a better way, but are you looking for it?

Have you heard of a paradigm shift? It is a scientific term that is defined simply as a proven way that something works. Because of its dependability, it is used by many with no adjustments. But there comes a time when an individual change must be made. The time is now to remove everything that is no longer productive to and for you. It is time for a paradigm shift. There are paradigms for every activity of life. But it is a wise person who makes the change in paradigms when one particular way of living is no longer bringing the desired results. In Dr. Phil McGraw's 2003 book "The Ultimate Weight Loss Solution," he talks about an overweight man who was working on losing weight. There was a big problem, he loved to eat. You may say that this is obvious, but this was not the main problem. He was the manager of a grocery store; his whole life was surrounded by food. He may have gone to college or had special training to be a grocery store manager, but this career could have been the death of him.

The paradigm shift here would be that being a good grocery store manager was going to have to transition into another career. You may be thinking that this is a drastic change, but these are the kinds of changes that make success be successful. You must be able to change the way you think when what you think is no longer working.

This is what I want you to do now about the word rest. Although the example of God resting on the seventh day was in the Old Testament, it makes sense for you in the 21st Century. God is not a man. God is the God of the universe. He controls it all, everything you see and don't see. For you to understand how God operates, He would have to restrain Himself. Restraint doesn't make sense for God, but it makes sense for you. There is no way for your finite mind to totally understand an infinite God. God created time so that you could function in this life in a specific order. Eternity is a term incomprehensible to man. But when it is compared with time and lined up against days, it makes sense. He made time on the third day, but what is a day in God's sight? God is in eternity. He has no beginning and no ending.

As an all-powerful being, God constrained Himself to finish his creation in six days. He could have thought out the process and created it all in a moment's time. But since He loves us, He held Himself back and gave us an example. This example is where we live today. He gave it to the children of Israel in the wilderness (Exodus), but they rejected the gift. God made a whole generation of Israelites, that complained in the wilderness, died in the wilderness, although they were on their way to the Promised Land. They never made it there. Everyone from the age of twenty and up died in the forty-year journey. The trip from Egypt to the Promised Land should only have taken twelve days, but it ended up lasting a generation because of all the complaining. **They wanted bread, God sent bread; they wanted water, God gave them water; they wanted meat, God sent meat.** Their clothes nor shoes ever wore out. They cried to be delivered out of slavery in Egypt and God did that. When they reached the wilderness, they said that at least in Egypt they had onions. There was just no satisfying them. Their trust in God did not exist. Moses begged God not to kill them like He thought He might do. They provoked God in every way that they could. The question is are you more concerned with being satisfied or thriving in God's plan for your life?

I want you to understand the rest that God has planned for you. The caravan of believers was led by Moses. Moses was a faithful man and wanted to lead his people out of bondage. Moses himself got so mad with the children of Israel that he did not even make it to the Promised Land. But God sent Jesus to lead us into the Promised Land of Rest. Moses was a great leader, but Jesus is greater because He is the Son of the living God. I want you to understand this principle because it is important to the fact of living in the rest that is promised to you. Moses was a servant of God so that he could be an example to you of what God was promising you for the future. But Jesus was not a servant but he is a son over the house that you as a believer are a part of. The way to remain in this house is to keep believing in all the promises that God has given you. You can't just believe today and then drop it tomorrow and start complaining. You must keep believing. When you open your heart to hear and receive this knowledge you need to hold on to it. It is God speaking directly to you. God spoke to the children of Israel but they did not have the faith to believe. In resting, God will speak, but in order to be successful beyond the rest you must believe what He speaks.

God was upset with the children of Israel because He had so much for them, but they did not have the faith to receive. They did not know how God was operating. I want you to embrace the way that God operates. If you grasp the point that your troubles are just temporary then you can live in the rest that He created just for you. God, as great as He is, did not need to rest on the seventh day; He wanted you to follow the spiritual order. He completed everything for you and wants you to know that the seventh day was created for you. He created man on the sixth day and then the work was done. The day that man lives in is the seventh day. It is the day of rest. You are in that day now.

Life has a way of throwing you off track. When the refiner's fire gets really hot, you start looking for a way to get out. You start making your own plans of escape. It may be extremely uncomfortable, but it is going to make you better. God is simply looking for His reflection in you. This is a lifetime process, but the fire is not continuous. How can God know if you are progressing if He does not allow you to make your own decisions in your own life? I know you and I both know that God knows everything. God's plan is to show you yourself. When you get a fire break and travel far from God, you will run back if you know how good the refining process has made you. You do not know what is in you until you have to deal with situations and interact with others. Where do you think all this deceitfulness of life comes from? None of the things you worry about will matter if you lived on this earth all by yourself.

The sonship of Christ is shared with us

when we accept this rest (Romans 8:17). The only thing that keeps you from this promised rest is unbelief. You can only live in this state of rest by practice. It is a daily test. When you come face to face with this place of promised rest, it will readily be available to you again when you travel far away from it.

No matter your situation, if you can remember that nothing catches God by surprise, you can live in that peace. Your life will be a testimony for someone else. Stop working to figure God out and just rest. When you enter this state of rest, you stop working to save yourself. Those trying times are the refiner's fire, rest in them. If you can learn how to rest in the fire, what can you do when you come out of the fire? You have nothing to do in this life but rest in God's benevolent care. The work that you must put into action is the training of learning to rest.

You cannot fake this peaceful lifestyle. If you are not really resting, then God will know and you will definitely know it. You know how it feels to worry. But worrying is not a function for man. It is the cause of a lot of sickness and heartache. Jesus is here waiting for you to come with a heart full of desire to rest. It is okay to take a nap in the middle of the day, if you can. It is okay to go to bed at 8:30 p.m. What is wrong with a vacation where there are really no plans, only a delightful hotel room overlooking the beach? Embrace this paradigm and enjoy this secret. Do not neglect this precious promise that was prepared for your enjoyment. **He desires to give you rest and is concerned about you.**

"Let us therefore come boldly unto the throne of grace, that we may obtain mercy, and grace to help in the time of need." (Hebrews 4:16)

Rest does not mean STOP.

You must be able to change the way you think when what you think is no longer working.

DEGREE FOUR

FRIENDS IN THE FIRE

I believe that you are familiar with the writing called "Footprints." I want to talk to you about that here in this chapter, hoping that it will encourage you to stop fighting when the fire gets hot and finds company to share in times of trouble. I need to keep reminding you, as I do myself, that God is in full control. He knows exactly what is happening in every moment of your life. Again, nothing surprises God. As soon as you begin to walk in this knowledge, it will be the time when your life will become much easier to live. The most troublesome times in life are when there is turmoil around and you feel like no one understands where you are. God always knows where you are and He is always standing right there waiting for you to acknowledge Him.

The writing "Footsteps" tells the story of a man who had a dream that showed all the time periods of his life. His life was portrayed as a walk along the beach with the Lord at his side. He looked down and saw two sets of footprints walking side by side. After the last scene of his life traveled by, he looked back over his life. A troubling scene came into view. He noticed that during the most painful times of his life that there was only one set of footprints in the sand. Being the spiritual man that he was, he asked the Lord how being left alone could have been the right thing at his most vulnerable times. God answered him without hesitation. He told him that the rough times when it seemed he was alone were times when he was being carried. God would not allow him to carry himself through the storms of life. Up in the arms of Jesus, the only footsteps making impressions in the sand were those of the Lord.

You have probably seen this writing

hanging on the wall at someone's home or read it in a greeting card. This poem has been around since the 1940's, but just recently was attributed to a woman named Mary Stevenson. If you do not remember a single line from the writing, you will probably remember the thought that God carried this dreamer. This is the point that I want to emphasize here: God's benevolent care of you is clearly manifested when you are at your lowest. You would not be able to stand under the pressures of life if God did not take away all your burdens when you were collapsing under the weight. Thank God for His grace that sustains you when you would otherwise fall. No matter how close your friends, family, and associates are, they cannot take care of you like God.

Are you around friends who you can depend on when you are in trouble? There is a story found in Daniel 1-3 about three young men who were down for each other. Their names are Shadrach,

Meshach, and Abednego. These three Hebrew boys lived in a society that did not worship God. Although surrounded by idol worship and witchcraft they held fast to their faith. The king at the time, Nebuchadnezzar, decided to build a huge gold statue. His herald made a decree that every day when all kinds of music were played that all people in the land would bow down and worship this gold image. Those who refused would be thrown into a fiery furnace.

It was soon discovered that the three Hebrew boys were refusing to worship this false god. Brought before the king, they were unified in their answer to the king. They would not worship this image and said that even if their God did not deliver them out of the fire, it did not matter, they knew that He could. Into the fire they went. Way back in the Old Testament, you could see Jesus walking around in the fire with them. They came out of the fire with no burns and didn't even smell like smoke.

Their faith had sustained them. All three joined forces, went in the fire together and came out of the fire whole.

Who are your friends? "One who has unreliable friends soon comes to ruin, but there is a friend who sticks closer than a brother." (Proverbs 18:24 NIV) A faithful friend does not run from you when you get in trouble, they are there for your troubles. God cannot resist unity. In Genesis 12, you see the story of the Tower of Babble. Because the people were determined to unify in disobedience they could not be stopped. God had to mix up their language so that they could not understand one another. Unity is powerful. I ask you again, who are your friends? Are you around people who can support you when the fire is turned up to 1200 degrees, or are they running because they are afraid to get burned? God does not need them to help carry you but if you are going to have some they may as well be good ones.

Are you a good friend? When your friends are in the middle of adversity, can they count on you? Or are you a fair-weather friend? There is a scripture that is not often quoted, "...bad company corrupts good behavior." (I Corinthians 15:33) What does this mean? No matter how you were raised or how you trained yourself to act, who you hang around will reflect in your actions. The second phrase of Proverbs 18:24, "...a friend that sticks closer than a brother," is not talking about a person. This scripture is referring to God. But still God expects us to have and be a good friend. Our relationships are how unbelievers know that we are believers. (I John 4:18). The love you show to each other is proof that God's love is in you.

I will not tell you that remaining friends with people in difficult situations is an easy task, but if you draw back when times get rough, you are weak (Proverbs 24:10). This is one of the main reasons that choosing friends must be done with wisdom. What happens when you need someone to rescue you? Friends are created for adversity. You can always go to a movie, restaurant, concert, etc. with an associate, a coworker, a fellow student, neighbor, cousin, sister, etc. But what happens when you are in desperate need? Who is there for you? This is the purpose of having good friends. You need someone to go in the fire with you like Meshach. Do you think Shadrach would comfort you when you are down? He walked in fire with you, of course he will. You need someone to stand up with you for what is right. Can you count on Abednego? He did not bow down to the king's gold idol, even with the threat of being thrown in a fiery furnace.

Then there's the problem of those bad company friends. Run from them! You may end up in the fire that you and your friend set. No matter how nice you think you are; those friends who just do not do right, do not think right and do not act right are bad for you. Hang around a friend every day who is a chain smoker, even though you do not smoke. Your chances of getting lung cancer or some other breathing problem are much higher because of the dangers of second-hand smoke. This is the same principle as that bad company friend. You know who they are. You have convinced yourself that you are good for her and that you can help him. I am telling you that this is the wrong answer. All your proper manners are going out of the window. You will sit and wonder why your mind is wandering into areas that you never thought of before. If you are not influencing him, then he is definitely influencing you.

You will meet people that will need what you have. They may turn into good friends but there will be many that are only there to get what they need from you and move on. Do not try to make every associate a friend. You can tell a real friend. He is down with the fire. He is there saying let's go, our God is able!

I have been there. I understand about those fair-weather friends and I know about those friends that are down with the fire. I have also heard about those innocent victims of user friends. They are not really friends, but only there to get what they can. When their time in your stuff is up, they move on. There is a middle-aged lady who had been in this dilemma for over forty years. She could never understand why she'd have one good friend but was hurt in many of her other friendships. After counseling, she was made to realize that she was always the giver in these other relationships. She had the "messiah complex." This gracious lady was always there to rescue others. When she needed rescuing, her user friends were nowhere to be found. She had to come to realize that these in and out people only wanted what she was offering, not her. They were not the "in the fire" friends.

Learn how to have a life of simplistic giving. If you are always around friends who are takers, then ask yourself are they really your friends. Open yourself up to revealing some weaknesses to these "friends." If they stick around, then maybe you have an in the fire friend. If they run at the first sight of trouble, let them run, and cut them off; or guard your heart and know that they are not friends but associates.

There is no one like our God who carries us when we cannot carry ourselves and there is nothing like friends who love us enough to walk with us into the fire, even at 1200 degrees!

Do not live in your emotions, live in your FAITH.

The original plan is still GOOD.

DEGREE FIVE

CHANGE STATE

Transition is a word often used but the process of transitioning is often neglected. When in the fire, you will experience many transitional moments in your life. Transitions occur mentally, emotionally, spiritually, and even physically. Transition is not limited to these areas. It can also be experienced in your relationships, finances, health, career, as well as your geographical location.

According to Merriam-Webster dictionary, transition is defined as a passage from one state, stage, subject or place to another. Simply put, transition= change, and change results in something new.

When you are in a state of transition, the first thing that must be refined is your mind. Anytime your mind is in a state of flux (which is all the time), if it is not renewed, it will remain in the state that it last visited.

Romans 12: 2 gives us a warning about keeping our minds in the last state visited.

1. Warning. "And do not be conformed to this world…"

2. Here's what to do. Act, "but be transformed" , meaning transitioned and catapulted or brought into a new mind.

3. Next is the purpose. "…so that you may prove, show fruit, that what is good, acceptable…", or what you accept and reject according to how you value the purpose of who you are, the perfect will of God.

Let's pull out the word transition: The scripture in Romans 12:2 ("But be ye transformed") and in Isaiah 43:19 suggest to us that Transition is present. Transition being present in your life signifies to us that spiritual progressing and success is available to be in your life now.

You're at a threshold for transition which

means the intensity that must be exceeded for a certain reaction to take place is available within you.

For example, in order for a man to ask a woman to marry him, intensity of his love must increase to the point that causes him to have a certain reaction. That reaction will equal a proposal.

Maybe you found yourself in a financial need in your life. The intensity, or the extreme pressure of needing more finances causes you to go after better education or apply for a job you didn't qualify for. It even pushed you to release a financial seed because you know in the release it will open up the continual flow you need financially. You need the condition to change, so you act in what you think or know will bring change into your life.

It's so wild to me, because I have done this numerous times. When we need help, we ask God for help, and that is what we should do... but then when He answers, we ignore Him. Why do we do this?

There are times in our lives when we need to live at the next level of our destiny. The only way we experience this destiny shift is by implementing the direction that God gives us for our lives. In the direction is the strategy to get to our next level of destiny.

The truth is, we do not like the feeling of change. We have a perception that says it will be too hard and that change takes too long. So what do we do? We ignore God, and we try self-direction, which gets us nowhere. When we choose our ways and not God's way, we usually end up back asking Him for help anyways. So why not implement His ways first and save ourselves a lot of time and pain?

Mathew 19:26 says, "With man this is impossible, but with God all things are possible."

If you were to make a list of everything in your life that is impossible for you and then compare it to a list of things that are

impossible for God, there would be no comparison. What makes transition hard is doing it without God. When we do life with God then all things become possible. The hardest parts in life are trusting, listening, and acting on God's direction with consistency. Consistency is defined as unchanging in standard. This means that no matter what transition you find yourself in, if you keep the standard or combination of trusting, listening, and acting on God's direction, you will find yourself getting through the fire quicker and with total success.

You might have encountered many downs, but this is your moment to start encountering the ups. If you have never been excited about your life before, now is the time to get excited. Your moment to shine is here, your time to fulfill your destiny is now, and the life that God created for you to experience is surfacing through the fire.

There is a particular person, function,

and area in your life that serves as your motivation. Relationships, finances, health, ministry, travel - one of these or multiple areas will remind you that to keep pushing when the fire gets too hot.

Push through each degree until you can see your dreams become reality. Keep transitioning up and don't stop. With each level you will discover some of the greatest parts of your design. **Keep your thoughts towards God and never let go of hope.** Hope will get you through the tough times and remind you there is more for you in life then where you currently are right now.

Hebrews 12:29 says that Our God is a consuming fire. God's presence is manifested and His voice is heard when we are in the fire. Why? Because He is right there with us.

What does it really mean for God to be an all-consuming fire? Let's first define consuming. Consuming is defined as to use up, take completely, engross, or total take over. And fire is defined a refining, purification, destruction; to ignite, blaze, or inflame with passion and zeal.

The fire of God comes to do five things in transition:
1. Refine
2. Ignite
3. Protect
4. Take vengeance against your enemies
5. Affirm His acceptance of you

Your transition from degree to degree is to shift your from natural living to supernatural living. For example, refinement comes into your life to change you from sickness to healing, from poverty to prosperity, and from confusion to clarity. It brings a new way of living that benefits you. **God wants you to upgrade from an ordinary life to an extraordinary life.**

So what is your part in the transition moments? First, keep the fire burning by being in constant devotion and worship to

God. You must think of worship like the flames heating the coals. Romans 12:11 tells us to not burn out, and to keep yourself fueled and aflame. Next, work on getting the ashes out of your life. Ashes represent sin, selfishness, defilement, corruption, and the list goes on forever to include all nature of negative.

Basically, get rid of anything that keeps you from moving forward in your purpose. We are not perfect, nor will we ever be, but the heart to pursue the best level of living is what God is searching for. Remember: He has forgiven you of your sins, but the enemy is always there trying to push you ten steps back. So stay focused and ask God for help in the areas of your life that seem to be hard to do on your own. A fire always burns it brightest and hottest when it is free from ashes.

Last, prepare yourself for the next degree of heat. In my home, you cannot just walk up to the fireplace and tell it to turn on. I have an original fireplace in my home and so in order for it to carry the fire, it must be prepared properly. You are similar to my original fireplace: you must also prepare for your fire to be lit properly.

First, prepare your pit, which is your heart. Next, you must gather the wood which is the word of God through prayer, praise, and worship. Last, you must constantly throw out the ashes, poke the wood, and add new wood. Exodus 29:38-43.

If you want transition to equal something new in your life, ask God to turn up the degree of heat.

Turn up the degree of HEAT.

DEGREE SIX

P2= POSITION + PURPOSE

I want you to understand that there is value in pressure. **Pressure always reveals what is being concealed.** Oil is not produced until an olive is pressured and the oil that is inside of it has enough weight on it to extract it. Oranges produce freshly squeezed juice when the shell is peeled and the pressure is applied to it. Pressure being present in our lives reminds us that there is a treasure on the inside of us that can be better utilized externally than internally. These internal treasures include gifts, talents, skills, and abilities that enhance our lives. Pressure is where real purpose shines and real strength stands firm. Pressure is the true test that asks, Are you going to give up on the challenges, or are you going to thrive into your purpose?

The common thread in all the chapters

of this book is pressure and progression. If you handle pressure the right way, you will see yourself progressing and your life expanding in purpose and achievement. Pressure is a sign that you're moving forward or that it is time to move and make a change. Pressure indicates that purpose is right on the line and if you allow for the pressure to process thoroughly, you will step right into your destiny. Pressure is a sign of value being revealed.

Pressure in your marriage causes change and value to take place. Pressure in your finances causes value and perspective to be placed. Pressure in your business causes progression and success to be revealed.

Some of us that are under pressure, the heat right now is not because God is punishing us or does not see value in us, but rather it's because we have met the conditions to enter into the refining process in this time in our lives. We have been handpicked to move forward in our purpose. We must have the right perspective on this pressure so that we will manage it correctly, and the true value of who we are will be revealed.

Pressure is defined as the push exerted on a specific object or area. When you are feeling pressure in your life, the majority of that pressure comes from what I like to call the detachment stage. When you are ascending in your purpose, it's critical that you detach from what was and attach to what will now be. This means you have to detach from old habits, mindsets, and emotional entanglements that no longer serve your purpose and the strategies that used to work but no longer do. Sometimes we are holding on to past relationships and bad habits (such as eating or gambling). Some of us are holding on to pride and guilt and shame. As long as we hold on to those elements in our lives, we will not be able to come out of the process as intended or purposed. But if we choose to detach and attach to the new things God is bringing into our lives, the results we are looking for will show up in our future.

If you keep making bad choices in the way you deal with your finances, then you will not be able to reach the financial goals you are setting for yourself or live in the surplus of finances that God intended you to have.

If you continue to make the wrong decisions and choices when it comes to your family and your spouse, then you will continue to have a relationship that reflects those decisions.

If you continue to hold on to pride, guilt, or shame, then you will never be open to allow someone to help bring change into your life. You will be stuck in the same cycle and you will not progress.

The pressure should equal progression. Remind yourself of this statement every time you feel like the pressure or the heat is too consuming. If you are not progressing through the pressure, then you are not changing, and if you're not changing, that means you are staying in the same place you entered the fire in. If you are not moving forward and progressing, then you need to reevaluate the choices that you're making. Seek God and allow Him to direct you, and listen and be obedient to the instructions.

Hebrews 4:12 says, "For the word of God is alive and active. Sharper than any double-edged sword, it penetrates even to dividing soul and spirit, joints and marrow." This scripture is saying that the word of God is alive and active. That means that it should be actively working in your life. The scripture also says that it is sharper than any double-edged sword. That means that no matter what you have going on, or how bad you think the situation may be, even if intensity of the pressure has increased, the word of God can cut and withstand anything that you're up against.

So the question becomes How do I get through the pressure and win?

The first thing is you need Faith. The Bible says that without faith it is impossible to please the Lord. You yourself are not what brings the change. Rather, it is the faith that God will bring change through you is what brings the change.

You need to educate yourself. If you're trying to learn about money, read a book on how millionaires think. If you need change in the bedroom with your spouse, read a book on intimacy and sex. If you need progression in your business, read material and study how successful companies were built. Knowledge comes from education and information, and allowing the Holy Spirit to give you wisdom on how to use what you obtained.

You need to shift your you're your surroundings and your sounding board. Everybody can't go where you're going, or help you understand where you're headed. You're asking your grandmother who manages her social security money on how to manage your multi-million dollar contract - that doesn't add up. We love grandma, but she cannot be a sounding board for you. Grandma doesn't qualify.

Second, you need to become active. Keep moving in the process. Don't stop, don't look back, just keep moving forward. Put action to your plan. Remember: it's not about everything being perfect - that's God job. You just have to be active and He will keep guiding your every move.

The last and most significant step is filtering the last bit of impurities so that God can see His reflection in you.

Sometimes we go through pressure, then all of a sudden we have peace. We feel like the pressure has lifted and we've made it through. But then all of a sudden we start feeling the pressure again.

I want to encourage you to not give up

at this point because that's just the last degree of heat before you are removed from the fire. This is the point to make sure that nothing is left that can taint or change the purpose that you're walking into.

This is a time for you to keep pressing forward and to not fall back to old habits. This moment is for you to find peace in the pressure. Peace that God has a great plan for your future, a resolve to know that everything you encounter or reencounter will work out for the goal you are pressing to achieve.

A peace you must rest in is to know that the God that lives in you, that is holding you up and clearing a way for you, is the God that already overcame all.

The Bible says in Isaiah 26:3 that God will keep you in perfect peace, just keep your mind and your trust in Him.

The ending to the pressure in your purpose is revealing the true value that was in you. Know that it doesn't matter where you started, it matters where God places you. And understand that your promises have been sealed by the life and blood of Jesus Christ.

When you feel like you can't go any further and that the pressure is too much, tell God. Start going through all the reasons why you can keep going, and He will energize you to keep going. Remember that it's temporary, and you will come out of the pressure. You are being positioned for your promise and that process takes commitment, faith, perseverance, prayer, and an attitude that says I will not stop until I get to the top.

Make a reminder list. This list will give you focus in times of doubt. You will feel like quitting at times, but your reminder list will display all the reasons why you started, what you're working to accomplish, what sparked the need to change, and the desire for next level living. Remember that you will not break, just keep pushing through. You were designed to last, and you were created to handle the heat with God. The Bible says that God will not put more on you than you can manage. So whatever level of pressure that you're at, remember, you've got this!

As long as you're willing, God will bring in the rest. The strength, the wisdom, the patience, the right support – everything! - you need to walk into your purpose.

Expect the proof of Who God Is and the proof of your purpose to show up in your life.

Get rid of the triggers in your life that are keeping you from shifting into a new place.

Progression comes from the words that we speak, the thoughts that we think, and the atmosphere we create around us.

Be totally consumed with who God has created you to be. Being consumed with who God created you to be will create a passion that is on fire for your purpose. You will begin to bring change to your thinking and actions, and it will result in amazing experiences in your life.

Command your life to respond to your VALUE.

DEGREE SEVEN

SURFACE

Have you ever wondered how a diamond is discovered and/or how it is made?

A diamond can only be formed in high temperatures. In order for a diamond to be formed, it must be subjected to a combination of pressure and heat.

The heat results in the diamond's texture or roughness. It is one of the factors that makes it unique. Diamonds are built to withstand both pressure and heat. The heat strengthens the diamond so it doesn't break during the creation process.

We are as special as diamonds. And we, too, go through pressure moments in our lives that we make us feel pressure and heat. But we are created just as strong and as brilliant as a diamond – and just as strong.

Your life at this moment should remind you that you are designed to withstand some incredible heat and pressure. Just take a look at yourself. You didn't break, you might be a little dusty, but you still have shine on you. You're even still standing on your own two feet. Standing up in strength. And the scars you have gotten along the way just enhance your beauty. Nobody but you could have gone through the heat.

You know what makes you valuable? The story of where you come from, where you've been and what future you're getting ready to surface to. The durability of your faith and the courage to hold on to your faith makes your value greater than rubies. Nothing but God's son Jesus Christ could even compare to the value of your life. **You are something awesome and the quicker you figure that out, the future you have been looking for will show up so fast that you wish you would have**

come into this knowledge sooner. The good thing is you know now, and God wants to show you off to the world!

God wants to transform you to something that is universally admired. The physical residue of what you went through will not be marked on you, and the clarity of your value is getting ready to be displayed for all to see. Including you.

There are two things that surface when you start to come out of the refiners fire.

First, you release the value by releasing your design. The more of you that is implemented into your life (I'm talking about the real you, not the masked you), the greater your design will be seen in the new refined you. Remember: a diamond is more valuable the more transparent it is. If you can see your reflection in your diamond, than you have a pretty valuable object in your possession. The value of your intelligence, creativity, strength, love, bravery, and so much more will be revealed.

Elevation is the second thing that surfaces in your life when you come out of the refiner's heat. Heat does not break you, it elevates you. When heat is applied to a diamond, the diamond is then pushed to the surface to be revealed.

God is not making you, He is unveiling your next level of life. He wants you to live, but you must receive who you are – the real you - to receive the new level.

There are some areas in your life that are still in the rough stage. Those areas must be refined so that the value of your design can show up.

In the depths of the earth's core, down deep, is where you find diamonds. That lets me know that in the depths of my situations, in the deepest parts of the depression, doubt, fear, sickness, there is

Value
Clarity
Strength
Durability

You know that each of these qualities is there, but they aren't seen until pressed out with heat. It's not until a blast from the earth's mantle dislodges the rock that the diamond begins to surface. You have allowed who you are to sit in the hidden parts of dirt, circumstances, and everything else negative holding you back, and it takes trauma of "growing through" an ordeal or a shattering encounter to blast you out – this is how you get to who you truly are.

The dirt that holds the diamond is like the strongholds that hold down our purpose. Strongholds modify our behavior. They blind us and create illusions to keep us looking to the past so we won't receive our future!

We must stop breading our tomorrows with we speak about today. We must stop being ambassadors for our past and start leading and living as we are already in our future.

"National Geographic" says that

humans cannot even survive the depths and heat that a diamond goes through to be formed. That is why it is so awesome that we are part human and part spirit, and that the spirit of God lives in us. The Bible tells us that Deep cries out to Deep. So what you humanly can't do on your own, let the spirit of God get you there.

What God is doing now means it's going to be greater than what was then. A new hunger for God is here now and ready to surface in you. A new passion for ministry is here now: let it rise up in you. A heart for your family, a discipline and vision for your business, a hope for greater health are all surfacing.

I'll ask you: Don't you perceive it? Can you sense it in your environment, can you feel it in your spirit? This feeling will increase in time, keep surfacing, and soon you will start seeing the light.

Giving won't be a problem because you know the new money, the greater seed, not just the increase, but the overflow is coming now.

His image is shining through you. Maybe you feel like you left your identify all behind you and it's stuck in the past. Maybe you feel that you've lost your anointing. Maybe you feel that your purpose has no definition to it anymore, and your dreams are fading. Keep surfacing; it's all going to show back up in your life and this time it'll be here to stay. You jumped in the fire with God, and He chose you for this moment. You're ready to do it with God. **No more doing life alone, it's you and God all the way.**

When Moses went back to free the children of Israel in the book of Exodus, what made the difference, what brought the increase, was that Moses did it with God. On his own, Moses was unable in some areas, but where we are weak, the mightiness of God makes up the difference.

Surface. Command your life to respond to your value, to the image of your

Creator, to your speech, and to your faith.

No more withholding yourself from your life. Don't worry about the condition of your life; conditions breed opportunity to bring what is desired into reality.

I started the list for you, now you take it and add to it, finish it, and experience the greatest level of your destiny you were created to live. Pray to the Lord:

    Refine my relationships
    Refine my finances
    Refine my faith in You God
    Refine my mind
    Refine my health
    Refine my value of who I am
    Refine my dreams
    Refine my courage

There's more than where you are right now.

Know that Jesus is the ultimate refiner.

You are not damaged goods. You are not just another piece of metal, unvalued and label unworthy. You have been chosen for the fire, your true value is surfacing, and your life will never be the same.

Summed up in a twist on Oswald Dykes' English Proverb, "One mans' junk is always God's treasure."

Turn Up the Heat and Surface!

ABOUT THE AUTHOR
ILKA MURRAY

Location // Atlanta, GA

Affiliations // AMM + BossLady Network Life Back On

Author // Ilka Murray

Community // 1love, United Way

Tags // Faith, Ministry, Women's Ministry, Community, Global Stage, WomanAlive, Millennials, Cultural Diversity, Generational Diversity, Conferences, Authors, Creatives

LIFE BACK ON
Faith + Lifestyle Brand
Global . Creative . Faith

Taking every area of your life to winning status.

Ilka Murray is a practical and inspirational teacher committed to encouraging people from all backgrounds to push through layers of hurt and pain, and take every area of their lives to winning status. She calls this Life Back On. She is creative, intelligent, bold, and audacious woman of Dominican heritage. While she has excelled in every area of her life, she is most proud of her accomplishments as a daughter, sister, friend, wife, and mother. She has two vibrant children. Ilka's a fresh voice in business and ministry is contributing and evoking excitement and anticipation to experience life as God designed in the lives of people around the world.

www.ingramcontent.com/pod-product-compliance
Lightning Source LLC
LaVergne TN
LVHW051848080426
835512LV00018B/3137